973.4

READING POWER

Westward Ho!

THOMAS JEFFERSON AND THE LOUISIANA PURCHASE

EMILY RAABE

The Rosen Publishing Group's
PowerKids Press™
New York

10/03

Published in 2003 by The Rosen Publishing Group, Inc.
29·East 21st Street, New York, NY 10010

First Edition

Book Design: Michael DeLisio

Library of Congress Cataloging-in-Publication Data

Raabe, Emily.
Thomas Jefferson and the Louisiana Purchase / Emily Raabe.
    v. cm. — (Westward ho!)
Includes bibliographical references and index.
Contents: Thomas Jefferson — The Louisiana Territory — Lewis and Clark
— Exploring the West — Opening up the West.
ISBN 0-8239-6499-X (lib. bdg.)
1. Louisiana Purchase—Juvenile literature. 2. Jefferson, Thomas,
1743-1826—Juvenile literature. 3. United States—Territorial
expansion—Juvenile literature. 4. West (U.S.)—Discovery and
exploration—Juvenile literature. [1. Louisiana Purchase. 2. Jefferson,
Thomas, 1743-1826. 3. Lewis and Clark Expedition (1804-1806)] I. Title.
E333 .R123 2003
973.4'6—dc21
                                            2002002932

Contents

THOMAS JEFFERSON

Thomas Jefferson was one of the people who helped America win its freedom from England. He also helped write the Declaration of Independence. On March 4, 1801, Thomas Jefferson became the third president of the United States.

United States in 1801

Northwest Territory

Mississippi River

VT
NH
NY
MA
CT
RI
PA
MD
NJ
KY
VA
DE
TN
NC
SC
GA
Part of MA

New Orleans

Atlantic Ocean

Gulf of Mexico

President Jefferson was also a teacher, scientist, inventor, and musician.

Thomas Jefferson played an important part in setting up the first government of the United States of America.

THE LOUISIANA TERRITORY

At the time Jefferson became president, the United States went only as far west as the Mississippi River. The Mississippi River was very important to American farmers. Farmers used this waterway to send their cattle, hogs, grain, and produce to market.

Farmers brought their goods down the Mississippi River to the port at New Orleans. From New Orleans, the farmers' goods were sent by boat to other places.

New Orleans was part of the Louisiana Territory, which was owned by France. Farmers needed to ask France for permission to store their goods at the New Orleans port.

In 1802, President Jefferson decided to ask France to sell New Orleans to the United States. On April 30, 1803, President Jefferson sent James Monroe to France to buy New Orleans and the land around it for $10 million.

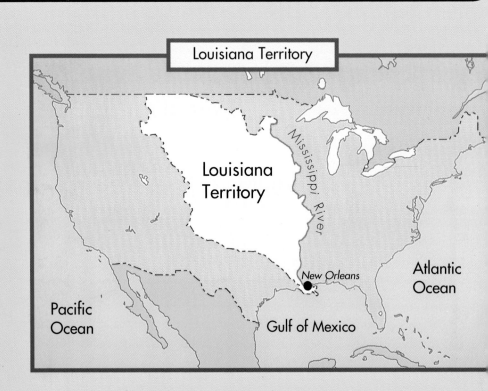

Louisiana Territory

Louisiana Territory

Mississippi River

New Orleans

Atlantic Ocean

Pacific Ocean

Gulf of Mexico

James Monroe became the fifth president of the United States. He believed that no European country should try to take land in the Americas.

Instead, France sold the entire Louisiana Territory to the United States for $15 million. The sale of this land was called the Louisiana Purchase. The Louisiana Purchase more than doubled the size of the United States.

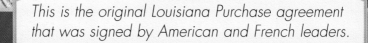

This is the original Louisiana Purchase agreement that was signed by American and French leaders.

Now You Know

The United States paid about four cents an acre for the Louisiana Territory. This set an example for getting new territory by purchase rather than by war.

France surprised James Monroe (left) by selling the whole Louisiana Territory to the United States.

LEWIS AND CLARK

President Jefferson needed people to explore the land of the Louisiana Purchase. He hired Meriwether Lewis to lead a group of explorers into the wilderness west of the Mississippi River.

Jefferson sent Lewis to the University of Pennsylvania for a month and a half to learn about animals, plants, rocks, minerals, and medicine. Lewis also learned how to use the stars to guide him on his trip west. This is Lewis's drawing of a bird he discovered while exploring the land of the Louisiana Purchase.

Lewis's group was called the Corps of Discovery. Lewis chose William Clark to help him lead the trip.

Lewis and Clark had no maps of the land of the Louisiana Purchase. The Corps of Discovery was the first large group of people to travel across the country to the west coast of America.

Lewis and Clark took 30 men with them. These men were soldiers, boatsmen, carpenters, and blacksmiths. Some of the men could understand and speak Native American languages. The group also took medicine, food, weapons, and tools for studying plants and animals.

Meriwether Lewis

William Clark

"A great number of the natives came with corn, beans, and moccasins to trade, for which they would take anything—old shirts, buttons, knives . . ."
— Patrick Gass, one of the men who traveled with Lewis and Clark

Lewis and Clark spent $669.50 on gifts for the Native Americans in the Louisiana Territory. They wanted to give gifts to the Native Americans as a sign of friendship. The gifts included beads, ribbons, mirrors, cotton shirts, and kettles.

EXPLORING THE WEST

Lewis and Clark's trip began on May 14, 1804, in St. Louis, Missouri. They made their first winter camp in what would become North Dakota.

Some people in the Corps of Discovery kept journals of their travels in the wilderness.

Lewis and Clark met a Native American woman named Sacajawea (sa-kuh-juh-WEE-uh). Sacajawea was a member of the Shoshone tribe. She agreed to guide the group along the Missouri River.

Sacajawea, whose name means "Bird Woman," acted as an interpreter between the Shoshone people and Lewis and Clark. She helped the explorers trade for things, such as horses.

As they explored the land of the Louisiana Territory, Lewis and Clark made notes and drew pictures of 122 plants and animals that they found there. These plants and animals had never been seen in the East. They also made the first maps of the land west of the Mississippi River.

Many people in the East had never seen a buffalo, which was a common sight in the West.

Lewis and Clark came across many animals, such as the grizzly bear, during their trip west. Some of these animals had been unknown to people living in the eastern parts of America.

Opening Up the West

The Corps of Discovery returned to St. Louis, Missouri, on September 23, 1806. Their trip had taken two years, four months, and ten days. They had traveled 7,689 miles across plains, mountains, and rivers.

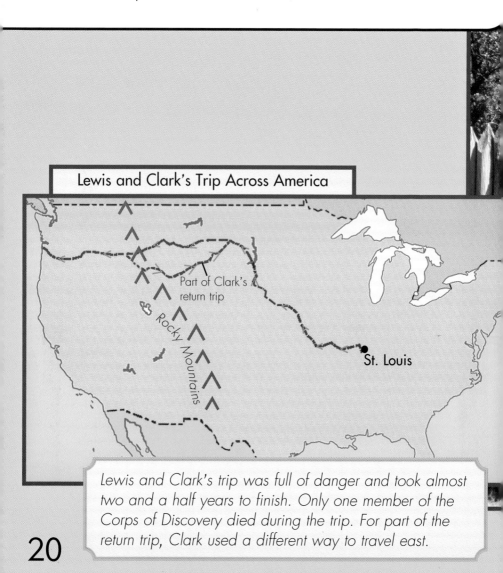

Lewis and Clark's Trip Across America

Part of Clark's return trip

Rocky Mountains

St. Louis

Lewis and Clark's trip was full of danger and took almost two and a half years to finish. Only one member of the Corps of Discovery died during the trip. For part of the return trip, Clark used a different way to travel east.

The purchase of land by President Jefferson and the work of Lewis and Clark made it possible for Americans to settle in the land west of the Mississippi River.

This fort was built to look like Fort Mandan, in North Dakota, where Lewis and Clark stayed during the winter of 1804–1805.

Glossary

blacksmiths (**blak**-smithz) people who make things out of iron by heating and hammering it

corps (**kor**) a group of people brought together for a special job

explored (ehk-**splord**) searched for new places

freedom (**free**-duhm) the state of being free

interpreter (ihn-**ter**-pruh-tuhr) a person who changes the words in one language to another language

permission (puhr-**mihsh**-uhn) when someone is allowed to do something

purchase (**per**-chuhs) something that is bought; to buy something

territory (**tehr**-uh-tor-ee) the land and water that is controlled by a country or state

wilderness (**wihl**-duhr-nihs) a place with few or no people living in it

Resources

Books

Lewis and Clark for Kids:
Their Journey of Discovery With 21 Activities
by Janis Herbert
Chicago Review Press (2000)

How We Crossed the West:
The Adventures of Lewis and Clark
by Rosalyn Schanzer
National Geographic Society (1997)

Web Sites

Due to the changing nature of Internet links, PowerKids Press has developed an online list of Web sites related to the subjects of this book. This site is updated regularly. Please use this link to access the list:

http://www.powerkidslinks.com/wh/tjlp/

Index

B
blacksmiths, 14

C
Corps of Discovery,
    13, 16, 20

F
freedom, 4

J
Jefferson, Thomas,
    4–6, 8, 12, 21

L
Louisiana Territory, 8,
    10–11, 15, 18

M
Monroe, James, 8–9,
    11

S
Sacajawea, 17

W
wilderness, 12, 16

Word Count: 476

Note to Librarians, Teachers, and Parents

If reading is a challenge, Reading Power is a solution! Reading Power is perfect for readers who want high-interest subject matter at an accessible reading level. These fact-filled, photo-illustrated books are designed for readers who want straightforward vocabulary, engaging topics, and a manageable reading experience. With clear picture/text correspondence, leveled Reading Power books put the reader in charge. Now readers have the power to get the information they want and the skills they need in a user-friendly format.